I0756321

FINISHING LINE PRESS
www.finishinglinepress.com

Shadow Boxer

poems by

Martin Cossio

Finishing Line Press
Georgetown, Kentucky

Shadow Boxer

ISBN 979-8-89990-488-2 First Edition

Publisher: Leah Huete de Maines
Editor: Christen Kincaid
Cover Art: "Shadow Boxer" by Hugo Antuna, ha! studios
Author Photo: Robert Nuñez
Cover Design: Hugo Antuna, ha! studios

Order online: www.finishinglinepress.com
also available on amazon.com

Author inquiries and mail orders:
Finishing Line Press
PO Box 1626
Georgetown, Kentucky 40324
USA

Contents

to, and with a final ten-count for, Joel Lamore,
the man who taught me form

Tale of the Tape

after Eloisa Amezcua

Martin Cossio	NAME	Martin Cossio
212	WEIGHT	212-
34	AGE	34+
5’9”	HEIGHT	5’10”
Left: 75” | Right: 74 ¾” (flabby forearm)	REACH	Left: 75” | Right: 74 ¾” (metal and screws)
Orthodox	STANCE	Southpaw
Mexican American	NATIONALITY	American Mexican

Shadowboxing

I hear the ping-ping of the bell
and no one who is fully sane
can fathom why. This bell to box
is like a tic that can't be seen

an internal clock I feel at work
each time kids say they have a "sub"
in front of me, each time I drink
and sabotage my sober self

then force myself to take the L.
I hear the ping-ping of the bell
and rise up from my stool to fight
with cops, or in a parking lot

then go back home and celebrate
a swollen eye with more Bud Light.
I hear the ping-ping of the bell
and wake back up, put make up on

then go to face a new school site
before I sit back down to write
my coach's voice inside my ear.
This bell to box is like a clock

a tick that can't be heard or seen.
I hear the ping-ping of the bell
this tic developed over time
spent doing time and putting in

the time it takes to win a prize.
I hear the ping-ping of the bell
and no one who is fully sane
can fathom why, at thirty-four,

a rising poet would start to box.
I hear the ping-ping in the ring
where one is heard as well as seen
because I live the metaphor.

Plan B

When your fiancée tells you not to come
in her, but coming with her, you stay inside
of her because you thought, or hoped, she meant
the opposite and had decided to succumb—
when making love becomes an argument
and she spills truth, like she's the one who's drunk,
by questioning if you're fit to be a father
and your starter home becomes a sterile room—
when the plan you had (pre-Covid) to join as one
and, like a cell, divide in two becomes Plan B,
and she reveals that to adopt is her plan A,
and you realize that was growing inside of her—
the decade you've spent investing in each other
becomes the life you will not have together.

Learning How to Dance at 34

I never understood dancing
I admitted to my girl.
The few times I danced in my twenties
I did it
with my lights out—

if dancing were a mating ritual
I'd prove unfit
to propagate.

But now I'm in a boxing gym
poised in front of a mirror
like a dancer in a studio.

Our coach has just walked by
and said my form is off
again.
I look at my feet and think
about geometry, the coordinates
of my fighting stance.
If my back foot
can't hold a 45-degree angle
will my timing
even matter?

For months now I've tried to find a rhythm
with myself and still
I can't hold a proper stance.

I'm back at square one
my feet are stuck
but I wanna figure out the steps
to this dance.

I wanna learn to move
on my toes
like Lomachenko
who learned ballet before
he learned to box

learn to shuffle my feet
like Muhammad Ali

and bend my hips
like "Iron" Mike.

I want my feet to lead
my lanky arms
and me
in circles
around my dance partner.

I wanna lose this beer belly
and see the abs
I've wanted ever since
I started doing sit ups
while watching wrestling
as a boy.

I want my girl
to be able to reach into my shirt
and feel the definition
on my stomach
and know I have core strength.

I wanna be able to say
I've finally learned to dance
so I could dance a special dance
with her
and be able to place my hand
on her stomach
feel the circumference
of our prize.

I Pondered Lonely as a Cloud, on the Clock

If killing time were a crime . . . then thinking this
would be attempted murder, 'cause Time can't be killed
or even bothered. It stands still, like me, a sub
still, growing older where the kids stay young. One asks,

"What time is it?" . . . I say. Then think, interrogate
the question: Does that make grammatical sense?
What is "it"? What time is what? And when will it be
for us? Or is the question, What is time? The "it."

Time is the murderer, the one now killing *me*
and forcing me to watch, to face it day by day,
though it's not there . . . and only this conundrum is:

To murder Time in self-defense would mean to kill
myself . . . and to attempt to murder Time would be
a crime—for which I'm here, already doing time.

Shadowboxing with a Mirror

There's something in my groin
that keeps me going. I tell myself
something has to come of this
if only blood and broken cartilage—
sh-sh—

You never liked it anyway—
sh—
What breaks—
sh-sh—
can be rebuilt
But you
don't have insurance
—sh-sh-
-sh—
The metal in your arm
won't make you stronger
—sh-
sh-sh—
I'll switch to southpaw
Head can't take
these kinds
of shots—*sh-sh-*
sh-sh

Keep fighting
from the outside
no
keep working your way in

their livers feel your hook—
shh—
the world will open up

Coach Pedro said one orange is all the water you need in a day,

and I picture a boxer on his stool spitting out the water his trainer squeezes into his mouth. Imagine having to have less of something good. I still struggle to have less of the bad. But now I carry around a smaller bottle, am almost in fighting shape; still fighting to make super welterweight. And lately one of the other coaches, Coach Juan, has been going around offering us pugilists orange wedges from a Ziploc. Twice he's approached me—retired on a folding chair, staring out past the punching bags and shadowboxing mirror to my undecorated classroom—and offered me citrus I accept with still-wrapped hands. In well over a year, those are the only two interactions I've had with him. I don't know if he keeps us in mind when cutting oranges, but I'd like to think those wedges, more than a show of affection, are his way of communicating approval, the way certain men only know to do. And I imagine he looks forward to distributing the wedges, not as a trainer but a fellow fighter who at one time may have found a lifeline in an orange wedge, a mouthpiece suckled on between late rounds. And I have to believe those wedges were his way of saying he's been watching me from the ring, that he can tell I have a different kind of fight ahead of me, in a different kind of ring, and that a bit of pulp is all I need to keep going.

Coach Robert said the body is a perfect machine—

Una máquina perfecta—as I looked him in the eye and considered the science involved in seeing. *No other machine more perfect,* he continued in Spanish, a realization from his days as a bodybuilder. Nowadays I don't defecate much. Sometimes I don't go at all, and I'm not necessarily eating less. But I had regained five pounds despite my continued resolve. *But what does the mirror show you?* Now that I stop to look, I see my torso transforming itself in real time. He asked about pushups, my diet; I hit him with a list of what I'd had that day: two eggs cooked with avocado spray, two strips of air-fried turkey bacon, an eighth of an avocado, some grilled chicken, a scoop of white rice, handful of edamame, one whole orange. He did some mental math, estimated the calories. Said my body was responding to what it knows I'm going to put it through, that before, it would eliminate what it knew I didn't value—I recalled how my college biology partner said I looked pregnant, "Respect yourself"—and I began to understand how pro fighters can put back on so many pounds after weighing in before a fight. He pinched my remaining belly fat, gave me a percentage range. Asked with his hands, *Out of ten friends, how many are where you are?* My first thought was, I don't have ten friends. Smiling at my delayed reaction, he told me what to do next: more cardio, first thing in the morning and on an empty stomach, and four sets of post-gym pushups, followed by a cold shower. And I realized gaining back five pounds when I only had five more to lose actually meant I was winning the fight no one thought I'd survive.

Coach Ruelas said a boxer is like a robot:

a trainer programs you to throw a combo and you go practice it ten thousand times over until you find yourself standing over your opponent, wondering what you hit him with. If I could give myself a moniker, my AKA would be "Mexican Machine," "Mexican" because Mexicans march toward battle—*Mexicanos al grito de guerra*, the battle cry beginning of Mexico's national anthem. The less time there is to think the better... Boxing is human chess. A battlefield. Described as the art of hitting and not getting hit. But there is no not getting hit. Some fighters will take two to land one. A Mexican will take three and not retreat. And all that rattling of the skull eventually leaves you punch drunk, like the "Schoolboy," Bobby Chacon, who dreamed of chili dogs and lost his queen to suicide after promising he'd quit but couldn't. Boxing was her idea. Muhammad Ali would "rope a dope," pin himself against the ropes to tire out his opponents. He developed early-onset Parkinson's, what finally allowed him to slow down. But having done his talking in and out of the ring, he held an indefinite smile. They called him the "Greatest." He called himself Muhammad Ali and refused to go to war with an enemy who never called him a you-know-what, a chess match that spanned three of his prime fighting years and cost him his heavyweight title. Now he's referred to as the "Greatest of All Time." I asked the old man what they called him. *Gallito*, "Little Rooster," he said. I wondered if it was more because of his stature or his gamecock eyes, claws he pointed at me once while at close range. Unlike writing, boxing is a young man's sport. Unlike boxing, training is a gambler's game. Ah, humans and their pastimes.

Coach Pedro said it takes balls to be a boxer,

not because you have to learn to take a punch, because learning how requires discipline, completion of the basic training you sign up for once it clicks—the clock. During drills, the *come on, weaky boy; do it, do it; you're going to be a boxer, not a Zumba boy* then going home and not treating yourself to a comforting meal. Like during Lent, those days of fasting, smaller portions. Giving up TV, and now, for good, Bud Light. "Iron" Mike moved in with his trainer, Cus, sat at a dinner table where no one else was Black. He became the world's youngest heavyweight champion. Coach Robert says if you want to be a champion, you have to train like a champion, usually as we're upside down against a wall enduring the weight of our bodies. I can hold out the longest (probably longer than him) and sometimes, after he finishes enunciating *tiime*, I keep holding on, like a penitent on display. He says the trick is to position yourself as vertically as possible. Once locked in place, I stay still, including in my head, like I have no choice. Like having to kneel in front of a wall as a boy. Coach says your body must obey your mind, not the other way around. I tell myself I asked for it, remind myself my body isn't mine. And maybe that was the problem, understanding one's body is borrowed. Because I couldn't own myself, I resolved to rage against myself by worshipping excess. Now I sweat and shake in handstands instead of while withdrawing in bed. Holding on, trembling, I focus on the floor, inches away from my face, and take it one second at a time as if my life depends on it, because it does. They say your body is a temple. But a temple is built from nothing.

Coach Robert said you have to visualize yourself doing it first,

the pull up bar a rung within my reach
reminding me of when he paired us up
facing each other and placed a disc cone
between us just outside our reach: He said
the next thing was easy—high knees
and on his cue, we'd reach for the disc.
Whoever snatched it before the other won.
Easy. You just had to want it more
than your opponent. I was up against a taller
guy with as much muscle as I had fat.
But then I understood it was a mental
exercise, that boxing was more mental,
for the mental and mentally strong. And I
told myself muscle weighs more than fat.
You're closer to the ground. He's already
gassed. Look, won't even make eye contact.

To punch a bag requires imagination,
the ability to see a moving target swinging
back at you while thinking on your toes:
you pop him with a power jab that slows
him down—slip, uppercut—or wrap around
its armless frame, preventing him from throwing
in the pocket; you even take a punch or two
that knock your head back, bust your nose,
then switch and stand behind a peekaboo
high guard, and in the final 30 of the round,
go toe to toe, foregoing caution—action
for the fans, like at the closing of a bout:

you work the heavy bag   like you're trying
to pound something   into it, or something
out—as sweat drops spot the floor around
its legless frame: grey spots you picture red.

A boxing ring is the true American dream:
a level playing field where pugilists
compete by weight for standing in their class
and belts too big to keep around their waists.

To box in an American ring is the dream
for those who sacrifice themselves by pounds
and punch the rounds to represent their corner
of the world, transcend their social class.

An American dream comes true inside the ring
where a prizefighter who's been knocked awake
by getting put to sleep keeps dreaming big—
of rocking bling like boxers out the ring,
people hearing their extended name—
and keeps abstaining, training with their team,
daydreaming of performing for the nation,
capturing an audience's imagination.

Spring Cleaning

We gravitate toward the garage.
Dad starts organizing the crap
behind the couch, paint buckets
topped with tools and hardware,
hanging gas cans from ceiling beams;
I clear the coffee table—Mom splashes
the glass with diluted dish soap
from a bowl—and sweep
the open spaces: around the beer fridge
and treadmill we use as a coat rack,
new 60" screen and $60 Craigslist
stand, tagged up filing cabinets
with power saws,
mismatched chairs brought home
from side jobs then roll out the shop vac
and suction little piles
of crumbs and dog hair,
from beneath the chewed-up cushions,
a Rio Ranch receipt
or two,
whole *chicharrónes*,
even a LifeStyles wrapper; my fiancée
interrupts to talk about last night,
so I just pretend I'm not mad anymore—
my rottie pawing at the side door—
and help Dad move the couch back
so we can have more room
(and it can double as a dam
for the rest of the junk)
                                        —cause today
Derevyanchenko's fighting Triple G,
and they're gonna make a mess.

Wilder vs. Fury 3

for the fight fans

When Fury stuck the uppercut and Wilder hit the canvas
in the 3rd, it was the fifth time in 23 rounds
someone had gone down for the count. If you watch the tape
closely, after he gets up, looking half asleep
or just plain mad, you can see him shake his head
from a corner in his mind. But at the start of the 4th,
Wilder, who entered the ring wearing blinging armor,
already looked winded and wobbly.
And how could he not when fighting so hard
to win and avenge his only loss to a rival
like Fury who in their rematch, following the draw,
thrust him like a gale against the ropes
and flicked his tongue at his bloody earlobe. Yes,
having to put your mouthpiece where your excuses were
and fight for your flesh and blood and God
against a bigger man with the blood-drunk world around you
banking on you to fall again and not get up
is exhausting. Which is why—measuring Fury
with his left—when everyone heard the thud
of the Bronze Bomber's right implode on Fury's face
sending a visible shock wave down his haunches
and Fury stumbled punch-drunk onto the canvas
if you watch the tape closely, you can see Wilder
stop himself from breaking out of his bronze
and into a victory dance, and why only seconds later
after the six-foot-nine heavyweight got up
Wilder willed the British champion back down
to wait out the ten-count on his back and elbows
allowing the gravity of Wilder's power to sink in
before getting back up and being saved by the bell. No,
one can't underestimate a fighter's will to win.
But Fury being the undefeated Gypsy King
who doesn't stay down, he got his second wind
and by the 7th, Wilder's mouth was full of jam. And at the end
of the 8th, though visibly beaten, still
Wilder raised his glove before returning to his corner

because by then, winning meant something else
facing the fans of his actual blood, sweat, and tears
so he could hold his head up to his preacher father,
fiancée, sons and daughters, sisters and brothers
back in Tuscaloosa, meant using his unswollen
eye to stay in the fight against a seemingly invincible force
that in the 10th swept him with a gust—right
check hook—that brought him down to his knees
and in the 11th—stretched against the ropes—
with a temple shot that knocked him on his side
half out, and left him, for a moment, hearing stars.

During Physical Therapy, the Aide Checks My Pulse

Wrist wired to electric stimulation pads
(the arm, he said, connected to my heart)
and staring off into space and time, the present
past, imperfect tense   he pauses out in front
of me and asks again if I'm okay,
and I snap out of it—
                                        the twelve-year relationship
gone to waste
                          like the ovulation kit
I saw in her trash   engagement ring
I found in a petri dish
                                        I bought for her that time
we visited the glass museum I lived next door to
the Facebook memory   her holding up the key
to our turnkey
                          starter home   it glowing
in the foreground
                                beating heart
                                                    my pulsating
hand stopped squeezing   —and tell him yeah.

Living Up to My Name

Coach Albert said he was fast, on the bag, but that I had him, and then I did—in a fetal position against a neutral corner—before Coach Sunny called *break*. I had knocked his head gear out of place. His head felt hard against my gloves yet easier to punch than a bag. For the first time, I was sent to my corner. *Go.* I saw he was wounded, panting. Coach Sunny told him he had to finish the round and shouted instructions, but I followed them first. And every time he dropped his head, I hit it, like a piston, with my uppercut. (It's the punches you don't see that hurt.) Coach Albert said keep picking my shots but don't stand so square and showed me a counter combination, and I stood ready, repeating the numbers to myself. Before Coach Sunny got to know me in the ring, he nicknamed me "Professor," because I teach, pointed out a contradictory clause in their contract, not the "Mexican Machine" or "Computer" like I had fantasized about. I guess I've taught my first lesson. Keep your head up, Champ.

Read the following passage on the history of the name "Martin" then answer the question that follows.

In fourth grade, I punched a kid for calling me Martin Luther King. He didn't know I'm also a Jr.—the 3rd. I recall Mrs. Azuelime saying, "No one better color Dr. King black, because no one's black." Dr. King understood no one's white either; Malcom X, formerly "Little," saw Black soldiers and White devils.

I don't remember how my elementary school teachers, or my classmates, said my name. What I do remember is, in middle school, the red-head security guard with a British accent telling me "Martin" is English—fun fact—and the freckle-speckled Mexican girl that clowned on me by pushing in the tip of her nose. In high school, my childhood best friend, who started throwing "nigga" around like a pronoun, dubbed me Mart Dog. In college, non-Spanish speakers took the trochee from my name and restored it to an iamb, pronouncing it with an e the way my dad's white bosses and our black neighbors pronounced his. After telling someone my name, sometimes they'd bring up the sitcom and make a pronouncement of the pronunciation. At home and close to home my name has always been pronounced with the ping of a boxing bell.

Now when people ask for my name, I sometimes hit 'em with the jab of that lowercase "i". And when anyone asks how to pronounce it, I tell them it doesn't matter, because it mostly doesn't. Sometimes I feel like crossing out my name and replacing it with something original. Sometimes I think about passing it down.

What is the author's perceived identity? Choose the best Anglicized version of the name of this first-generation Mexican American whose poem you're reading.

a) [Mar-tin]
b) [Mard-in]
c) [Mart-'n]
d) [mar-Teen]
e) all of the above
f) none of the above

those confronted
with the question of my name
usually go with d)
which I find endearing
the correct answer
is anyone's guess

Acknowledgments

"Congratulations on a standout performance. How does it feel
to win your first professional fight?"

"San Ber-nuh-diinnnoooh. Your boyy maade it!

First off, I wanna thank everyone who bought a ticket to watch my debut—Anthony Pangallo, Felicity Landa, Yanira Monterroso, Rebeca Green, Leslie Bohn, William Cullen, Anselmo Garcia, Emily Pereira, Jonathan Tejeda, Hannah Bodnar, Heather Groezinger, Breeana Lozano, Jeffery Green, Kanani Sole, Patric Pepper, Andrea Gannon, Leonardo Rivas, Chris Jackson, Franchesca Guillory, Cynthia DeMone, Roberto Hernández, Xotchil Delgado, Andrew Navarro, Michele Guzman, Collin Mitchell, Andres Lara, Pamela Peté, who bought two;

special shout out to my ring girl, Dominique,
who bought multiple, and printed flyers;

thank you, Coach, Dr. Graham, for being the first one
and making me a primary source;

thank you, Cuz, for hooking me up with that cover
let's keep coming up together;
Danny, for your continued support, even after all these years;
Kelly, for buying the last ticket I had without knowing;

thank you, Matthew, Mike the PoeT, and Jill for taking the time
to write those invigorating words;

and thank you, IE Poets and UCRPD poets,
for all the insightful feedback over the years—

How does it feel? How do I feel?

Like I just got knocked awake.

Dad, this one's for you."

Martin Cossio is the son of Mexican immigrants who met in an English learners class in El Monte, California. He was born in East L.A. and grew up skateboarding and getting into trouble in San Bernardino, part of a region in Southern California referred to as the Inland Empire, or the IE. Martin has been awarded an honorable mention by Academy of American Poets and a summer residency by Sundress Academy for the Arts. His poems have been published by various journals, including *The Lyric, Modern Haiku, Inlandia: A Literary Journey,* and *Last Stanza Poetry Journal.* He was named the first national runner-up for Inlandia Institute's 2025 Hillary Gravendyk Prize. A graduate of UCR, Palm Desert's MFA program and a former poetry editor and copy editor of *The Coachella Review*, Martin teaches at a local high school, trains at a neighborhood gym, and lives in "the blade" with his xolo, Squintly.

www.ingramcontent.com/pod-product-compliance
Lightning Source LLC
LaVergne TN
LVHW090541110826
845146LV00003B/1217

* 9 7 9 8 8 9 9 9 0 4 8 8 2 *